The Day I Found God in a Pub

Antonia Lyons

To Warren, for lending me his voice while I found my own.

Special thanks

Deep gratitude to Leslie Harris for enriching my spirit and encouraging me to fly high, always; Geoff & Linda Hoppe, Lee Harris, Dr James Hollis PhD, & Tom Kenyon for reminding me what I had forgotten; the people in this book and all those who never got a mention but shall always be remembered. And to You, for being here now.

Note to the reader

Dear Friend,

If you are looking for answers or quick fixes that can make your life easier, I offer none.

Instead, I will share with you slices of everyday life, with her messiness and unexpected twists and turns. It is in the unpredictability of our existence, that we are often reminded of the gifts hiding within ourselves. We are all graced with the innate ability to see a new day and move through the ebbs and flows of life. This is the very miracle we look for in others, forgetting how it is always happening inside of us.

Gentle yourself, reading through each story. There is no rush. I have personally *channelled* the intro of each chapter, so you could take a little pause and feel the words. Let them speak to your heart. They will remind you that you never needed to fix yourself or your life, and that the story of one is the story of all.

With Much Love & Grace,
Antonia Lyons

Introduction

I have hesitated to share these stories; I have wondered how they would benefit the reader, considering I offer no easy steps to success or wealth. No word of promise for a smooth ride, as we journey through life.

I often feel that we are all desperately looking for something – anything – that would give sense to our time in this world. Even when we think we do, we usually end up taking a big stumble and go back to square one.

Let us just say it as it is: *LIFE IS NO PICNIC.*

Surely, we all have moments of fun, bliss and connection; normally they happen when things go our way. Nevertheless, in the middle of the night, as we fight with our demons, life often feels too dark for the light to ever shine again.

What gets us out of bed when we are tired and weary? When, after yet another fall, we are bruised and pained? What makes us bounce off even the worst of times? What keeps us going when all hope is gone?

Is it the love for our spouses and children? For our family at large? For our pets? Is it the certainty that God, *our God*, will make everything OK if we pray hard enough and offer absolute trust and devotion?

There comes a moment in our lives when we realise that the choice to carry on is ours only and not depending on other people or events. We stop searching, and we start living. As new stories unfold, we share them with others while listening to theirs. Our story-telling gracefully replaces the need for answers, as the words spoken weave a living tapestry that holds us and keeps us close to ourselves and everybody else. It keeps us in life. We no longer rush to heal ourselves or strive for perfection when we truly accept our part in such a fine masterpiece.

This short book, a collection of fourteen personal stories, is my homage to our *humanity*. As I wrote each chapter and revisited some of the events in my life, I was reminded of all the times I stood in front *of the divine* and yet was too engrossed in my constant search for 'something bigger' than myself to see that. Starting all the way in Italy on a hot afternoon and ending in a London pub on a busy Saturday evening, every story could be your story too. I have been a scholar of spirituality and personal growth ever since I can remember. I always had the sense, even when I was really tiny, that we were *more* than what we appeared to be. This knowing allowed me to forge a genuine interest in other people and their stories. Young and old, I always found fascinating, what they had to share. Even when they had no words to describe their choices and feelings, I could feel what wanted to be expressed. Growing up, I felt the call to use my intuition to offer those missing words through my writing. I started to write a blog about everyday life and everyday people, and their search for something bigger than themselves. Today, from my little corner in the City of London, I help people around the world reconnect to their own wisdom and *bigness* through my Intuitive Storytelling, which gives me the privilege to witness the ever-unfolding human journey.

I truly hope that you stay till the end and join me in toasting to us – you & I – for the stories we have shared and those we are yet to begin, as we slowly remember what went forgotten along the way.

Some journeys you must take alone, for
they may take you far.
Although sometimes, you may not
remember which way you came and no
longer see the path ahead.

EVOKING GRACE.com

The Search

Living in London often feels to me like some sort of personal quest. Millions of bodies rushing around all looking for something, even though they may not be sure of what, exactly. Whether that one thing is hidden in the ancient thoroughfares or in full display on the busy streets, it will likely be missed by the wandering souls who are too busy searching to see that often what they seek is right under their noses.

I landed in London one crispy autumnal evening, with no plans and one suitcase packed with hope and dreams.

I came to find the magic and belonging I had been craving all my life.

I grew up feeling *misplaced*. Even at a young age, I would often ask God why on earth had he dumped me in my town when there was a life waiting for me elsewhere. I was born in the south of Italy, where sandy beaches meet crystal clear waters, and the sun shines most days. Surrounded by a big family and good friends, I always had the painful awareness that sooner or later I would barter it all for the life I was really meant to be living, no matter how far that would take me.

In time, I have come to believe that we do not belong to a place or a person. But to our *calling*. Whether we call it Higher Presence, or simply destiny, we belong to what that demands of us and where it takes us. When we don't know what that is, *we are foreigners even within our own hearts.*

This alone is the one thing that requires us to walk a path seldom straight while remaining committed to our yearning for growth, all the same.

It is an ever-unfolding journey, which often takes us away from what is familiar and which we must embark on with great care and courage. We may not have words to describe what we seek, and yet we keep on walking with the hope of soon spotting what we've been missing all along.

In this city, where the old meets the new in a timeless fashion, many times I believed my search was over and many times I obstinately started it again. Just when I thought I had found what would fill my heart with joy and peace, I would instead feel the same old emptiness under a mountain of new creeds and practices.

Never quite content and always feeling as if there was yet another little treasure to discover, my hunt took me to hidden places where incense lingers forever in the air and peace is sold at a high price. I would spend entire afternoons in temples, esoteric shops, and fancy wellness centres in the hope of finally *getting life*. There I joined many *fellow questers:* professionals, housewives, young and old; we all were from different walks of life. Yet we all had one thing in common: the aching need to understand why we were here; the desperate belief that if we ever got that figured out, our days would stop feeling like a survival game. We all shared the desire to anchor ourselves in this life and stay; find peace within her many storms and hopefully, in time, learn to change the weather altogether.

But peaceful, my heart never grew, and questions always stayed way too long in my, very often, crowded mind. The magic I came to find here in London, always eluded me and I was never quite able to hold it and make it stay.

Come. Come and be here. Don't move.
Don't look away for you will not find me.
I am right here, where you cannot see me.
But you can feel me, always.

EVOKING GRACE.com

An Unexpected Guest

As I enter the room, a sense of peace comes over me while my mum and her old aunties silently sew some old blankets.

I like coming back to the house where I grew up and taking a little respite from the charming madness that is London.

It is a very hot and humid Italian afternoon; one of those when normally people will take a *riposino* or try and find solace by the sea.

Today though, the older women in my family have come together to repair a few blankets that have been passed on from generation to generation.

The three aunties have shared many stories and many tears. They often tell of their younger selves during World War II; the fear whenever they heard bombs going off, the hunger, and the hope that one day they would be able to leave it all behind. 'Did they?' I have often wondered. I always like hearing their stories, even if in time they have all started to sound the same.

What I like the most though is that they are here. Nothing has stopped those young little girls from growing into women and choosing life all over again. Touched by their dignity and composure, I often felt to ask what kept them going, through their painful memories and an uncertain future. What gave them hope now that they have all lost their beloved sweethearts and their children have moved away?

But these are not women likely to embark on deep conversations about the hardships of life. After all, older generations have learnt the art of keeping their upper lips well stiff and their tears to themselves. But they do not need to speak, for their piercing eyes and composed presence reveals the grace only those who have looked at life from both sides, possess.

This afternoon they are particularly focused on the task at hand: to *bring back to life* what has kept both the old and young in the family, warm and comfortable year after year. The shutters have been left closed so as to keep the heat out and my mum and her aunties are sitting in a circle in the half-lit kitchen. In silence, their hands elegantly move over the fabric, as if creating an exquisite painting. The needles pierce through the blanket and drag the silky thread, sounding like a gentle breeze.

Suddenly, I no longer feel the heat. The air in the room is now light and cool. Every sound has moved to the background as if echoing from another room.

While I look at each of these women, their

serene faces and skilful hands, I sense that the very thing we spend our lives looking for is right here. In that sublime quiet, I feel very close to myself almost as if I had just come back home from a long journey. My mind and heart are still, and I know God is here.

The God we pray to and worship, who is unreachable to most and silent to many, is moving right beside us in this room, suspended in time.

It is only when one of my aunties speaks that I abruptly come back to my senses and realise the enormity of what has just happened.

'Pass me the scissors, sleeping beauty. You sit there half asleep while there is work to do. Make yourself useful or just go and take a nap,' my old auntie sternly mutters. I smile to myself while she goes back to her beloved blanket: how often do we come close to grace only to be distracted by our mundane affairs?

So, we look for her all over, often embarking on a lifetime quest, which will always and only take us back to the same place.

Home.

'Nah, Auntie, needlework is not for me. I am heading to the beach, and I shall take a dip for you lot too, shall I?'

And off I go, leaving God with my sewing gang as I am not quite ready yet to stay with the unexpected although very sought guest. I still feel the need to let the *outside* world beguile me with its many attractions and complications before I can truly welcome the uncomplicated and quiet presence of the Divine. Mostly, I am not ready yet to accept that what I have been looking for as long as I can remember, was right there, next to me and searching is no longer needed. After all, who would I be without it?

Little people with their little laughter.
Chasing life with her big wings.
They catch her and then set her free, so
their fun game never ends.

EVOKING GRACE.com

The Day The World Changed Forever

It is a very slow Tuesday morning.

The sky looks particularly grey and dull, and I just want it to be Friday already.

Tuesday is often the time when we all wish our lives away and doing so today, feels particularly appropriate as I feel quite rushed and unsettled for no reason. There is definitely something brewing in the air. I am not quite sure why that may be, but I strongly sense that I will remember this day for a very long time.

Absorbed in the chatter of my active mind, I am suddenly awakened by the noise coming from across the road. People are gathering outside a pub crying and shaking their heads, and for a moment I wonder if the Queen has left her throne and this life.

Making my way through the crowd, I manage to see on a screen in the distance that what looks like planes are flying into some very high buildings.

The Twin Towers in New York.

No way! How can this be? It must be a publicity

stunt; something our fellow Americans are using to get the world's attention! Urgent questions suddenly crowd my worried mind.

My phone rings and it is my boss, sounding alarmed. He suggests I should get to work at once as it is not safe to be about right now because he fears this might be a worldwide attack.

Is there a plane flying into our skyscrapers too? Are we all going to die? Is the world ever going to come back from this? There is no stop to my questioning, while my colleagues and I spend the rest of the day telling one another old stories of bravery and resilience.

When I finally leave work, I start to sense a certain desperation within me. I do not know where to go. Today no place on earth could feel safe enough: something has just broken, and I am having a very hard time trying to process it.

Eventually, I get myself on an unusually quiet train, hoping that a cup of tea at home will sort me out. Instead, tears start to stream down my face and my heart aches in a way I have no words for.

Until Life speaks and says, 'Enough. Come back to me now.'

Around me, a small group of kids are staring at my face. And my painted nails.

'Excuse us, miss. Your nails are nice.' Their thick Irish accent and cheeky outfits make me wonder if these might be young travellers, probably camping somewhere nearby with their elders.

There are two small boys and three slightly

older girls all sitting opposite me and just giggling away. The most endearing and mischievous little faces I have seen in a long time; by their tiny frames, I can tell none of them are older than six. So much life in their eyes; so much joy.

While the whole world is being swallowed by a dark pain, these little rascals found my red nails amusing. In the end, no matter the tragedies we all face, there is always a big smile awaiting us some-where. Always. And we just get to choose, as we go along, whether to smile back or not.

While I sense my heart breaking still, I choose to be right there with my little friends, whose mums are watching us, clearly entertained, from the nearby seats.

I get my red nail polish out of my bag (yep, I'm an 'always have my essentials on me' kind of girl) and start to paint their little nails. Even the boys'. They are so happy and excited. Their little hands shake hard so the colour will dry fast, and they can show their mums.

I had not realised that the rest of the carriage had been enjoying the little show, and by now everybody was laughing. Every single person on there had to find a way to carry on trusting life and most of all, their fellow humans. Each one of us has the choice to give up hope or just sit in silence and remain present no matter the grief we are all feeling.

We are faced with the same choice every day, for such is our time here in this world. An endless dance between madness and grace. Today on that carriage, I did not choose. Life chose for me. Will I be able to choose tomorrow? And the day after? Will the girl who carries her nail polish around always come along, spotting the joy of the world through its tears? Will I always trust even when I do not understand?

Once I get home, I put the kettle on straight away; life is filled with myriad comforting pockets; tiny moments when we become still and watch the world from a safe distance so as not to be swallowed by whatever we witness and experience. I always love holding the warm mug in my hand while watching life go by, through the window. Today though, there are no kids playing hide and seek outside, nor mums calling out their names because dinner is ready.

Today, time has stopped. It has been demanded that all of us be with the enormity of what happened, knowing that the world as we knew it, no longer is. And as we pause, we acknowledge the stark reality that there is no going back from here. For there are things in life that change us so deeply, we can only go forward. Until something new happens, and we get to change a bit more. We get quite bruised and battered along the way. Nevertheless, each scar is a reminder of how life happens through events so seemingly contradicting, we are left to trust, as we walk on, that there is a place for them all.

Strangers in the night talk through their eyes for the world is too quiet to hear their words.

EVOKING GRACE.com

Sometimes We Cross Paths
Like Shooting Stars

I t is cold tonight, but I do not care.

Sitting on the stairs outside a popular cinema in west London, after a two-hour tear-jerker, I am sobbing uncontrollably, uncaring of the crowd coming out. My heart is broken; another love that never took off; another man I would never see again. And I am darn tired of trying to make it big in London. Who am I kidding? No one cares about this small-town girl here. The city will carry on just fine without me and my many stories.

It is getting late, but I do not want to go home. While the cold air mixes with my sorry tears and almost pierces my face, I watch life go by in the distance as if it is all happening in a different world; a world I may never be part of. My heart aches even more at such a thought, and I just cry harder while curling into a tiny ball.

It is at that moment that I sense someone standing over me.

'It looks like you could use one of these,' a young and distinguished man joyfully announces while holding a box of Krispy Kreme doughnuts under my nose.

I stare at his face, wondering if this is a prank. Was I on *Candid Camera*? Maybe he is filming a documentary about lost souls in London.

The stranger has very elegant features and, from the way, he is dressed and spoke, I can tell that life has been very kind to him. His big blue eyes are looking at me as if to say I am safe and I definitely must help myself to one of his doughnuts.

The refined gentleman sits on the stairs next to me and tells me that he is on his way to one of the beautiful houses there to have dinner with his old mates.

The pastries are to be his after-dinner treat.

He hands me his handkerchief and tells me, 'There is no trouble a cup of tea and good old cake cannot fix. In the absence of tea, the cake ought to be extra nice, of course.'

We sit on the cold pavement, the posh stranger and I, eating doughnuts while life carries on around us. He does not offer words that could dry my tears. Instead, he offers silence; his presence and time, and sweets. But he does not try to make it better for me. For he never could and because I can do that for myself.

In tending to others, we often try to take their pain away. We want to say the words that will write a different story. We wish to offer the very thing our unanswered prayers never gave us: the certainty that it will all be well. But our stories and prayers are seldom heard when trust and compassion are missing. It is our ability to truly accept others as they are that turns us into the angels they need. The ones who speak the quiet language of presence and compassion and carry doughnuts to sweeten the wounded hearts.

I say good night to the young man, telling him that I am feeling much better, and I should get going. Besides, his friends must be waiting for him. And their pudding.

'Please, take this with you.' The posh stranger wraps one of the doughnuts in a tissue. 'You may get peckish along the way. Let me call you a cab. I will be awfully worried to know you are all alone on the streets of London.'

I smile and thank him for the kind thought. Tonight, losing myself on those very streets is just what I need, for the demons we carry within, often turn into diamonds at night.

'I shall walk. A bit of fresh air will do me good. Thank you. You don't need to worry. I am fine, really.'

He does not insist, and he warmly wishes me good luck.

I watch him walk away, the posh stranger who carries doughnuts. I realise I never asked his name. And he never asked mine. Some people are destined to remain strangers and only briefly cross paths. Just like shooting stars, flying close up in the sky. They meet if only for one moment, to remind each other of the universe they once shared.

I let your hand go so you can walk on your own. But I shall stay close and hold your heart instead.

EVOKING GRACE.com

Life Never Stops

I am looking at my father's face, as he lies in bed in a very old hospital in Rome. The many tubes attached to his body are supposed to keep him alive until all his loved ones get here to say their final goodbyes.

I am looking for a sign that shows my father does not want to go after all; that he has chosen to stay in this often-heart-breaking life, no matter what it takes. I am looking at him while squeezing his hand. 'Come on, Papa`. You cannot die. Come on, Dad. I am getting married in three months. You are not supposed to die.'

He does not wake up and his hand never moves again.

The doctors tell us that it would be very kind to let him go sooner rather than later. Should we choose to keep his life support on, the quality of his life would be extremely poor. The man, who is still very young, is quickly leaving us, and I am pissed off.

When do we get to play God?

At what moment do we decide to end another person's life, whether that is our own parent or a stranger?

I should not be here tonight. I have a wedding to attend to, in three months, and I should be at home choosing flowers and cake decorations. Instead, here I am, and I have never felt so angry in my entire life.

'Screw you, God, you coward. Where are you when we need you to make a decision? Where the hell are you when you need to save the day?'

I am looking outside the window at a few patients and their loved ones in the little courtyard downstairs. Sitting on benches scattered around, I can hear their laughter while they talk away.

Will I remember my father's voice?

'Please, Dad, please, talk to us. We cannot make this decision for you. If you can hear us, please let us know what we are to do.'

We turned my father's life support off on a very tranquil afternoon, as the sun was going down and the red sky slowly turned into dusty pink. They say that at twilight we can *feel* our souls. The liminal times usually bring stillness and clarity, and we are more open to something bigger than ourselves.

Sitting in the small bar outside the hospital, life is still happening around me; people coming and going, the sound of the cars' engines in full swing, and kids' tiny voices echoing in the distance.

So much life, while I have just met Lady Death and I wish I had asked her a few questions. *Where will she take my dad? Will he ever come back? Was he OK and did he wish he still was with us? Mostly, I wish I had told her that it is truly unfair how she turns up uninvited only to find us utterly unprepared.*

And while the sky is slowly turning a beautiful pearly grey colour, the air suddenly becomes light and very still. Every sound is amplified, every smell comes straight into my senses, my heart's beat echoes loudly, and my mind is strangely quiet and yet never so aware.

I am alive. My father has just died, and I feel alive for the very first time in my life.

Everything around me moves graciously, while the man soon to become my husband and I slowly sip bourbon on the rocks, staring at each other in silence.

'To Papa` Andrea, the man I never got to know enough.' Warren says as he raises his glass, and his blue eyes almost pierce my heart.

'Let's go for a walk. It will do us good,' he thoughtfully suggests.

The ancient streets of Rome are busy, even this late at night. Myriad of tourists, slowly walk around, trying not to miss any of the stunning beauty of *la Citta' Eterna*. Picture after picture; everybody around me wants to capture this moment and make it last forever.

My father has just died, and life has not stopped. Does she ever? Could we ever ask life to halt if only for one tiny moment, so as to take another breath?

We arrive in Piazza di Trevi and are taken aback by the sheer majesty of the famous fountain, we sit by its edges, while the crowd around throws little coins in the water as per an ancient tradition. Everywhere I look, life has made her appearance again. Grand and unapologetic, she is at her best in this square where so many have wowed eternal love through the ages.

'Will you marry me?' Warren takes my hand in his. He had already proposed on New Year's Eve while fireworks lit up the sky and we'd danced the old year away. Tonight, his question surprises and yet deeply moves me.

'I do not want to waste time waiting for a perfect moment. This is as beautiful as it is ever going to be. Marry me and let's cherish this life together.'

I whisper, yes into his ear, as I hold his hand tight, never wanting to let it go while tourists and locals swarm around us. As their voices and laughter echo in the chilly February air, we sit closer, offering each other a silence that speaks a thousand words. Two grieving hearts celebrate the life that just ended and the one yet to begin, knowing that what happens in between is what keeps this world going.

No, life does not stop. We are simply asked to trust her. Even when our hearts break, for they will heal again. We tend to our heart's pain by allowing the very things our mind cannot grasp to naturally happen. In the end, we come to learn that joy and sorrow are never too far apart, just like life and death.

A man came and showed us a new way.
But those who are lost, seldom remember
to open their eyes.

EVOKING GRACE.com

The God We Know

Eating al fresco always feels like being away on holiday, even here in the heart of London.

Tonight, our local Italian restaurant looks particularly lively and inviting. The beautiful full moon up in the summer sky looks down, amused by the hungry diners, tucking into their pizzas while old tunes play in the background.

The party at our table are merrily tasting a selection of wines before dinner is served, happy to just sit back and enjoy the beautiful evening. We meet here once a month; six ex-pats who have now been living in London longer than they ever did in Italy. It is normally a small reunion, but occasionally, we take a couple of friends along to introduce them to this slice of Italy abroad.

I am quietly observing the man sitting next to me, making small talk with another guest. It is the first time he has joined us, and I cannot help noticing that he is already on his second glass of wine. Maybe I am being quick to judge, but I am

intrigued by the young priest who has recently
moved to London and seems to have gladly em-
braced what the city has to offer. His delicate features and stylish look make me wonder if the
priesthood was always his calling, or if he had been
venturing down a very different path before taking
his holy orders.

Our eyes eventually meet and through a very
big grin, the young and well-dressed man of the
cloth asks me if I am enjoying the beautiful evening.

'Shall I fill your glass, dear?' he asks while top-
ping up his again. He goes on to tell me how he
feels tired after house hunting over the last few days
and that this dinner was both welcome and very
much needed.

'I am staying with a school friend and her cats at
the moment. She has been very kind and would let
me stay a bit longer, but she also has kids, and the
place feels rather crowded at times,' he mutters
through his big, cheeky grin. 'Don't get me wrong, I
do not mind kids, but I prefer cats and I like my quiet,' he carries on explaining while happily sipping
his wine.

He is younger than me and shows a genuine excitement and anticipation for life, which is both re-
freshing and intriguing.

'Father, I thought you would be staying in a loft
nearby, like most of your predecessors at the
church. Was it not to your liking?' I finally ask half-
jokingly, hoping for a good story. The local parish
church is rather wealthy, and usually, the priests
get to stay in very good locations during their ser-

vice. Why would anyone give up such a luxury without a very valid reason? Is the young priest running away from something maybe? Someone perhaps? Is he in trouble? I am always amazed at how wild my mind can often run, with its millions of questions.

In a very strong accent, the chatty wine lover tells me of relocating from Scotland to this ancient part of London a year ago. He had been very excited to move and hoped to be deserving of such a great opportunity. He was filled with great plans and his newly found faith. Not long before becoming a priest, he had spent many years working in fashion, just like myself.

It was on the shop floor, in fact, that he had started to sense something that went well beyond what our eyes get to enjoy. All those beautiful clothes and accessories suddenly became just a means to reach something extraordinary and ineffable.

'God!' I proclaim feeling very proud of my observational qualities. 'You realised you had found God in your customers!'

'Maybe, but for a while, I thought I had lost my mind. I just wanted to sell a few nice dresses, make good commissions, and maybe find a boyfriend. I had never been religious; I had no language to explain what had started to move my heart. It was only when I spoke to a friend's friend that it all started to make sense. He was a priest himself and it did not take me long to accept that something was calling me, although I struggled to call it God.'

He is looking at me intently now. His glass is almost empty, but he does not seem to mind. I have a feeling that he does not easily share his story, so I'd better forget about the wine and show genuine interest.

'When I arrived in London, I was excited to be part of such an established congregation. I was told the parishioners were an integral part of our beautiful church, and I hoped I had found a new big family. It wasn't too long before I realised that I had a very different view of God & religion.'

'Oh boy, this sounds big!' I think to myself while I stare at his big, deep eyes.

'They wanted the rites and traditions. They wanted the candles and the statues, while I just wanted them to see that they are God.'

I need more wine.

Never before have I met a man of faith being so honest and clear about his beliefs. Above all, never before has anyone told me that *I* am God, also.

'They won't have any of that,' he says. 'They like their incense and prayers too much to even see that they are what they are looking for.'

And as we go through yet another bottle of wine, I just can't help feeling in awe of how incredible our human adventure really is.

I smile as I talk to this young man who likes his booze and men and has so much wisdom and joy to share. I have gone very quiet, mostly because I do not wish to spoil the sacredness of this moment. He carries on telling me that after raising a few eyebrows among the rather conservative and well-to-do parishioners, he had felt the need to move to the local hospital and attend to the sick and poor.

He was certain that among their suffering he would find fertile ground for his rather provocative yet sincere beliefs because it is often through our pain that we touch by hand our own divinity. He was quickly granted a transfer, which also meant that he had to move out of his beautiful loft apartment and find himself much cheaper accommodation.

Our pizzas finally arrive, and our deep conversation gives in to our appetites, leaving us both happy to enjoy our Margheritas in silence.

Later on that night, I reflect on my exchange with my new friend and how many, many, many years before, another young man somewhere in the world, had also raised a few eyebrows and pissed a couple of people off, so much so that they put him up on a cross and shut him up for good.

I smile, knowing that those who came to change the world often speak a language hardly anyone understands at first, and walk a path only a cripple has the strength to venture down before everybody else.

I have lost myself in the noise of the world, for the silence in my heart is too loud to welcome.

EVOKING GRACE.com

Some Gifts Are For Life

'I have something for you, Antello,' Dennis announces, while quickly going through his big pockets.

It is an unusually hot day here in London, but the man I have now known for a while, who still cannot get my name right, is wearing a big parka jacket. One of those that gives you the perfect excuse to fill the many pockets with whatever you can grab as you go along.

I am sitting on the pavement not far from the shop I work in, trying to get through my jacket potato undisturbed by the many tourists. Covent Garden Piazza is usually buzzing with buskers and people on holiday, and today the crowd is louder than ever.

'I have got you a birthday card. Here, read it,' Dennis carries on, while he hands me a scruffy envelope with his shaking hand. He seems to be genuinely excited and a bit proud of himself, and I cannot help smiling. The man who can hardly remember where he lives has remembered my birthday and while I open the envelope, he giggles nervously.

Hope it's Fun-Tastic.

Best Wishes, Happiness and all the Joys to you on your Birthday.

Dennis.

I am speechless for a moment because I don't know how to thank this man who bartered his old life for the streets. Will my gratitude be enough? Shall I offer him money instead? Maybe buy him lunch? Lost in a sea of questions, I forget to thank my thoughtful friend.

'Dennis, why is it that you live the way you do? I have never asked you before, and I thought you'd like to share that with me.'

Oh Jesus, there are times when I wish I weren't this forward and inquisitive. I should just thank him for the card and walk away at this point. Instead, I launch myself on a very risky mission. I want to know why this man who once must have been very handsome and whose face is now streaked with deep lines, no longer feels like he fits in this world.

Dennis goes quiet. His eyes start wandering around, and I just wish I could erase the last couple of minutes. We sit in silence for a while. A myriad of feet ring on the cobbles around us, while the buskers keep on playing catchy tunes to the excited crowd.

'I had a wife once; and kids. I had two kids, and

a beautiful wife. I also had a job. I was a teacher, wasn't I?' The man softly starts talking again.

'Wow, you were a teacher? I knew you were smart!' *Please be quiet, girl*, I beg myself.

'A history teacher. I taught kids, didn't I?'

I gaze upon the many young tourists running around us as if we weren't there, while Dennis goes on telling me that his wife had been the love of his life. They had been school sweethearts and married very young. 'She was beautiful, I tell you. She was beautiful, my wife.'

When she suddenly died many years back, he was struck by such grief that he slowly started to die too. Or at least, he made all sorts of attempts to follow his beloved lady.

'I could not be there for my girls. I just did not want to be here anymore.' His voice was now so low, I could hardly hear him.

'They never wanted to see me again after they found out I lost my job because I turned up drunk in class one time too many. They called me a selfish bastard. Maybe I was, but the pain, Antello, the pain was just too much. I could not save them from theirs.'

He has been sleeping rough for many years. Dennis actually has a flat somewhere in the sub-urbs, but he prefers the loud and unsafe streets to the unbearable loneliness of his place. He tells me that he hardly ever goes there as he no longer minds wandering around London at night. He likes it, in fact. He has met many people, and some of them have very good stories.

'What is a good story, mate?' I ask him, feeling slightly upset at myself for being so intrusive, and at life for being so unforgiving.

'It's the one that makes you forget your own, if only for just one moment.'

I reach for his hand, his trembling hand, and I hold it tight for a while. We stay on the stony pavement in silence, as life carries on moving around us. I have no words to offer the man who has made the streets his home. Nothing that would make him rethink his hard choice.

I just sit by his side, holding his card in one hand knowing that some gifts are for life.

The one reminding you of home, is the one closest to heaven.

EVOKING GRACE.COM

Seasons of Life

'Don't laugh!' I sternly admonish my husband.

'Why? This is funny. I have to laugh,' he is quick to answer back as he playfully winks at me.

'Please, be serious. And stop talking; you are distracting me.'

'How am I talking? You started it!'

On the occasion of the Winter Solstice, we are setting up a small altar in our kitchen. I like honouring the changing of the seasons; this year, I especially feel called to offer our gratitude, even if the world is upside down. I take *altar-making* very seriously because it is my way of telling life, 'I do not understand you, but I am still going to thank you!'

My husband, who is the *light-hearted one* in the house, usually ends up making fun of my seriousness and reminds me that sacred and profane have always gone hand in hand.

This morning, he personally collected a few bits in the local park while walking our dog. A swan's feather, a few conkers, and three small pinecones are now laid out on the white doily I carefully ironed earlier, and which was passed down to me by my grandmother. She always told me how, back in the olden days, women would crochet their days away. A simple yet effective remedy against the sickening of the heart, at a time when people were just told to get on with it!

Her words came to mind today and oddly feel very current, as I contemplate these unsettling times.

Early in January, an outbreak in China, of a mysterious virus, spread all over the planet within days. They named it Covid-19, although 'life as we knew it, no longer is,' would have sounded more appropriate. The global pandemic brought us all to a sudden halt, causing many to radically change their daily lives. Some people have been wondering if the extreme measures imposed to stop the virus from further spreading, were really that necessary. Others just love the opportunity of taking a long break from the world and having a good excuse for it.

However we may have been impacted over the last few months, we all share the shock of having seen our world stop while feeling both powerless and alone; for, often, no matter whom we get to share our space with, it is our own company we struggle to feel.

With my husband standing next to me trying to keep a straight face, I light a small candle, place it on the altar, and just close my eyes. I want this moment of praise to be perfect. I want *whoever* is up there to know that we, down here, cannot really understand why this is all happening. But we trust it will have a good answer when one day we meet again. If I say the right words, if I pray hard enough, will *It* hear me? Will *It* make all this go away?

'Thank you, Spirit. See you next season. Let's eat now...' My husband chirpily states as he makes his way to the dinner table. He happily tucks into the pie we prepared together earlier on, and his childlike enthusiasm for the pleasures of good food, as always, warms my heart. Thus, I am tempted to point out how disrespectful he has just been in rushing this sacred moment; I secretly admire his ability to keep it real. He has always had an understanding and acceptance of life, which is not found in the many self-growth books I have devoured. Nor in the healing programmes I have enrolled on, or the meditations I have fallen asleep through.

I have been wondering lately whether I really believe that our prayers and good intentions always save the day.

Do I trust that there is something much bigger than my small self, always ready to welcome me in its loving embrace? Or is my longing to connect to it, just a desperate attempt to avoid feeling my *humanness*? For no matter the spiritual retreats I have found refuge in, the invocations I have respectfully offered, and the altars I have carefully prepared, I am often at odds with accepting life in her endless contrasts. Surely all this tending to the matters of the spirit should guarantee a little safety from the constant storms battering our world; or possibly, change the weather altogether.

I watch my husband in silence while he enjoys our homemade pie, and for a moment, I envy his ability to live in the moment; savouring every morsel while sneakily feeding our dog under the table. *Little things in life*, he likes to call the small pleasures we ought to allow ourselves if we are to truly live this life.

In giving these up, we offer our repentance for being human. Flawed and feeling unworthy of mercy, we turn our attempts to find the divine in us, into the abdication of our own grandness. We starve ourselves of the very thing that gives us sustenance: the acceptance of life with the myriad experiences she constantly presents us with; and the quiet trust that, through them all, a new season always comes.

I suddenly remember being in our local pub early in the year, sharing a quiet drink before the first lockdown was announced in the UK. Winter was coming to an end, and yet both my husband and I sensed that spring would feel rather different this year. For a while, we sat in silence, lost in our thoughts in the deserted bar area.

'How do you sit there and drink while this life does not make sense anymore?'

'What do you mean?' My husband looked genuinely surprised by the depth of my random question. He put his glass down.

'I look at those like you, always so self-assured, acting as if you knew the secret meaning of life.

Nothing fazes you or surprises you much. In the end, a global pandemic may be just the same as the Christmas holidays; only longer and without the family drama.'

'And what's wrong with that? What would you rather have me do?' He looked genuinely curious and took another sip. 'Go on, tell me. What do you think I could do to make all this go away?'

'I know there is nothing you can do, but what makes you believe that tomorrow is still worth waking up for? How can you accept life without the need to, somehow, make her go in a different direction? Make her go your way?' I asked him tearily, hoping his answer would help me see how this unjust predicament had been caused by divine intervention.

'I always felt that life is just a random series of events. Some good, some bad, most of which don't make any sense, even in hindsight. It's just the way it is, always has been and always will be, from the womb to the tomb.' He held my hand while our dog jumped on his lap. Her little tongue gently licked the frosty pint glass in his hand, and my husband laughed out loud while hugging her tight.

'Every season passes in the end, my love. This shall go too as it came. And while we are at it, we will endure the grief and treasure the good moments. This is how the world turns, and you and I are not going to change that. But we can wake up in the morning and see if we missed something the day before. That is what keeps us going, even when nothing makes sense.'

We carried on drinking in silence, sitting close together while our dog was asleep between us. Sacred and profane, lingering in the air, always go hand in hand. This is how the world turns. This is life herself. Some of us make altars and light candles, others enjoy mundane delicacies, but we all wait for tomorrow to show us something new.

We are in open negotiations with life.
She'll let us see a new dawn and never tell
when our last dusk is.

EVOKING GRACE.com

The Young Man Who Walks Through Worlds

I t has been a quiet afternoon at the church where I have been volunteering during the pandemic.

Every day I greet both new and regular visitors while I sit by the main entrance. Today, though, I have been mostly enjoying my own company and have hardly spoken to anyone. When the church is empty, I love walking among its silent corridors. It brings me back to a previous life when I certainly made this my home and opened its doors to the less fortunate souls trying to escape the horrors taking place right outside. Through the centuries, many were burnt at the stake for their creed or fell victim to the plague or various diseases sweeping across London, making this their sanctuary to find food and hope.

Today, same as then, the suggestive and ancient church offers respite from human tribulations to all those wishing to pause and gain their strength again.

During my time as a volunteer, I have met many

people and heard many stories; the sudden pandemic has made us feel all a bit small and lost in a world we hardly recognise. Whether it is the lonely widow who hopes to find new friends, the cab driver who lights a candle every day hoping his business will pick up again, or the world-famous actor who lives across the street and has been praying here since a young age, everybody comes in with something to give. I gladly welcome their gifts and the privilege of witnessing how such a unique time in history is affecting us all.

'Excuse me, miss, do you know when this church was built?' the young man, suddenly appearing in front of me, asks loudly. I had not seen him come in, and I am quick to assume he must be a member of staff at the nearby hospital, because of the clogs he is wearing.

He looks up at the ceiling and while poking his head through the main door, exclaims, 'It is very old, innit?'

His eyes, deep and dark, are examining the Gothic architecture with wonder and genuine interest.

'Yes, it is the oldest church in the City of London, in fact!' I quickly reply, proud of the knowledge gained through my intensive training as a City of London tour guide, many years ago.

He looks at me for a moment and very casually asks me if I am religious.

His question throws me a little and yet I feel strangely drawn to the tall and rather confident visitor.

Do I tell him that I am a convicted sinner in the House of God, but I look for no redemption? Perhaps I should tell him of my days as an aspiring *altar boy*, which resulted in being ridiculed by all the other kids at Sunday school.

'I am not what you would call religious, but I have a sense of something bigger always being close by,' I calmly state hoping the young stranger will desist from asking any more questions about my creed. Over time, I have learnt to stay clear from conversations involving politics and religion, as they often ungraciously stir the hearts up, making us unable to accept anything that feels too different.

Trying to change the subject, I ask him if he works at the hospital next door.

The young visitor bursts into loud laughter and for a moment I sense his presence filling the whole porch.

'You are a funny one, aren't you, lady?' He seems to be very amused at my deduction. 'I am just a patient, and I came out for a quick walk. I shouldn't really but it gets stuffy in there; plus, I love sitting in the church when it's empty. And, if no one sees me, I'll go and grab a cheeky double cheeseburger in a minute.'

A patient? This guy, full of life and light, is staying at one of the wards next door?

'Oh, I am sorry, I am being rude. It is just that you look so...well...yes, you look so well to me.'

'I have leukaemia. I have been in remission three times, and I am waiting for a bone marrow transplant. Next week is the week and, after that, I am done with this shit. I have got my music to go back to and big plans for the future.'

I suddenly hope he stays and talks to me some more as I feel like I have known him forever. Maybe he also made this his home in a past life, when we both served the poor and sick in the name of a God we worshipped, regardless of the atrocities we witnessed.

The young man carries on telling me about his passion for music, and how he started to rap during his time in a youth detention centre, before entering a different kind of prison. As he tells me what it's been like to be in and out of intensive care for most of his adult life, I look for signs of the illness on his face. In his eyes.

I see none and when I look harder, I can't help feeling a sense of strength and excitement coming over me.

While it is hard to imagine what he has been going through, I am taken aback by how strong and bold he looks. Patients from the cancer unit next door usually come in looking rather pensive and pained; their faces stained by suffering and fear. I have often found myself in tears, hearing their stories. Their prayers are to a God they still believe in, despite their suffering, and who, they hope, will grant them the courage to carry on.

This guy is different. The light in his eyes is the light of someone who has seen something others have not. It is his own light and he has met it in the darkest days of his young life. He walks through worlds, knowing that one can only really be alive when death is no longer a stranger.

'Are you scared?' I ask him.

'Nah. It is not my story this cancer shit, innit? I am writing a different story; I am always *gonna* beat the crap out of it,' he firmly states in a typical East London accent.

I know he means his words as I have heard them once before. Many years back a friend in remission from a very aggressive cancer, told me that upon hearing his unfortunate diagnosis, he simply knew that was not his story. At that very moment, he had to make the quick decision to write a different one, and he never doubted for one second that he could.

The two young men both possess the same fearlessness. The type that only stems out of sitting long enough with our own demons, knowing that no one will keep us safe but ourselves. We become our own prayer, and we no longer look up to the sky.

As no other visitor comes in, I sit with my new friend in the empty church and, for a while, we share no words. We both enjoy the serene silence this place has been offering for nearly a millennium to the wandering souls in search of a God often hard to find and yet so very close.

A few months later, while casually surfing the net, I rejoice in learning that the remarkable fellow is indeed writing a new story for himself. He is on a tropical island, doing what he loves most. Surrounded by friends and beachgoers, the pictures show him entertaining the excited crowd with his music, during a party, under the coconut palms.

It's a world apart from the quiet alleys in the cancer unit he got to know too well. He has thrown himself into the life he sometimes feared losing. He no longer needs to hold on tight to her. The brave warrior who fought many battles, can now loosen his grip and trust he is here to stay. Not just a patient in remission, this young man can start making new memories while treasuring the days he came close to death. For he knows she is never too far and always going where life is.

These hands.
These strong hands have picked flowers
and held death all the same.
And hardly ever knew the difference.

EVOKING GRACE.com

The old man who watches
life go by

'lright?'

'Alright, John? How's it going, old gu-v'nor?' I say loudly, as I try not to get run over by John on his mobility scooter.

I see him every day, good old John.

He is 96.

East End, born and bred, he has never left this colourful borough of London; apart from when he was eighteen and boarded a train at Liverpool Street Station – destination *Dunkirk*. But that was World War II and does not really count, so John still likes to say that he never spent one day away from his neck of the woods.

'How are you today, John?' I ask, knowing what I am about to hear.

Old people like their stories, and perhaps by telling them all over again they hope to perfect them and, perhaps, discover something new. Or perhaps they simply don't remember, and in the end, they turn life into a long love story to reminisce with the world, time and time again.

'I'm alright. I'm always alright. I went to war, didn't I?'

Yep, here we go again. Same story.

'Eighteen, I was. Young innit? That's young.'

'Yes, John. That's really young. Were you scared?' asking the same question as the day before.

'Nah, we didn't know then, did we? We was young. They just told us to get on the train and then we were in France. Never been to France before. We even went on a boat. Never been on one of those before, either. Never been anywhere, mate.'

It's a crisp morning in November and this old fellow is wearing his heavier coat. He says it gets chilly on his mobility scooter, which was a present from his children after a bad fall the year before.

That day, I had spotted him from my window, walking in the snow. It was still dark outside, and John was probably on his way to buy his morning newspapers. Slowly, taking one step at a time, with the help of his walking stick, a small shadow advanced in the silent snow. He may well have just been walking in a green field. I simply couldn't tell.

'He really is unfazed by life this man,' I had muttered to myself, sadly aware that boldness often comes at a price.

He ended up being bedridden for a while after he had fallen right outside the shop.

That time, even stubborn John had seen how he might need a hand after all, although he still refused to go and stay with his daughter. The East End is the only home he has ever known; where both his late wife and sisters once were.

'Two, I had, didn't I ... two skins. They were lovely, my sisters. I used to wear their Alans as a young boy, 'cause we didn't have no bees, did we?'

'Sorry, what? Skins? Alans? Bees, John?' His Cockney habit of ignoring basic grammar rules and using rhymes shows how this neighbourhood has always been his whole world.

'Skin and blisters, sisters; Alan Wickers, knickers! Bees n' honey, money. I wore me sisters' knickers coz me old man didn't have no money. Ah, but it was good then, better than now. People were tough. Strong.'

He has parked himself in the same spot as every day; his red-poppy pin shines bright in the sunlight. Today is Remembrance Day, and, for the occasion, John was interviewed by the local paper early in the week.

'Look, I had all me medals on!'

He'd made the front page. 'War Veteran is East End Icon.' Not bad, old fellow. Not bad at all.

'You look lovely, John.' For a moment I pause and look at this man who once could not afford his pants yet soon learnt how that matters little in the end.

When he and his crew finally made it to France, he'd killed a man during his very first battle.

'I had to, didn't I? My hands were full of blood. I could smell it for a long time. But he was gonna kill me mate. It was him and me from these parts. We always looked out for each other, didn't we?'

When he came back home, John had his

medals, got married, bought clothes and his life carried on as though he had never left.

And the friend?

'He died, didn't he? He didn't have it in him. It was tough out there. All that blood; the cold. It was hard, wasn't it? He killed himself, didn't he? I went to see his mum when I came back. Tough. You gotta be tough.'

Yes, one has to be pretty tough to accept life's very unfair contradictions.

Often verging on madness, we are asked every day to dance with what comes our way with as much grace as we can summon; and with as little thought as possible, for, often, ignorance keeps us blissfully sheltered from those storms we cannot weather. As we move along, some things will hit us in full and others we will manage to dodge. Dancing our way through endless shades of infinite colours, we come to learn that we are all saints and sinners under this sky; and, often, the difference is invisible to the eye.

'Do you ever think of that man and your friend, John?' I ask him as always, never quite sure of what I would like to hear.

'Nah, no point, is there? You gotta be tough. What could we do? We was at war. Young, we was.'

We stay side by side in silence, watching cars drive past fast while angels and demons tango their way through the grey clouds. This is the last time I see John.

A week later, the little man, in the local shop, tells me that the old fellow has gone to stay with his daughter in one of the leafy neighbouring towns surrounding London.

'It ain't the East End, is it? These posh places all look the same. I am only going for a little while, just to keep the family happy,' John was heard telling the neighbours.

He does not come back: these days he can be seen freely roaming around the quiet and safe streets near his new home, as I learn from some of the local folks who pay him a visit occasionally.

Good old John. I often think of him on his mobility scooter. Watching life go by, just like a regular spectator at the local theatre. Front row and all seats to himself, never mind what show is on. Drama or comedy, thriller or musical, anything goes for the man who once stared death in the face. That day on the battlefield, he told *her* it was not his time yet and not to bother coming back any time soon. She must have taken his word for it and has been watching him from a distance ever since.

I see you. And in your eyes, I find myself again.

EVOKING GRACE.com

Smiling Eyes

'**M**orn'n!'

'Morning, kind sir!' It is still dark outside, and I am late for work. Not too late though to chat with Ken.

Like every morning, he greets me with a smile that makes me want to keep the whole world waiting so I can stop and take my time. Life is too short to be rushed through, after all.

'How's it going, young lady?'

'It's going all right, Ken. It's going all right. I am just tired of these early starts but let's not complain!' I am suddenly aware that Ken starts his shift at 5 am every day. He smiles and says that he knows how it feels.

I have not known Ken long. I remember one early morning, rushing down to the station, and late again for work. I had seen this man smiling at me while sweeping the pavement outside my building. I walked on but kept on turning around, still wanting a bit of that smile.

Who was that stranger? And why had he said

hello to me? Did I know him from somewhere? Was he crazy? Maybe dangerous? He could not be, though. Not with those smiling eyes.

The following morning, the stranger said, 'Hello,' again and smiled while I just lowered my head and muttered a half-hearted, 'Hey there,' suddenly taken aback by my awkwardness towards this man's lovely ways.

Yet his smile did something to my heart. What could that be? How can a perfect stranger move something in you and yet words fail you?

One morning out of the blue I went up to him, to the *stranger* sweeping pavements, and I introduced myself.

'Hi, I am Antonia, and I live there.' I pointed towards the red-brick building across the road. 'Do you work around here? I don't think I've seen you before?'

'Nice to meet you, Antonia. I am Ken and I maintain a few of the buildings on this block. How are you today?'

Why had I never seen this man before? How could I have missed this smile?

From then on, our morning chats became one of my daily rituals; little moments of undivided presence to what life offers me. Tears and laughter, all the same.

Ken tells me of his upbringing in the Caribbean, of being a young boy here in London, and how exciting and scary it all was. He tells me of the difficulties and of the great people he's met along the way. Joy and sadness always go hand in hand in life, but it seems to both of us that the world favours the victims it always creates; only to turn them into its own torturers in an endless and unkind game.

'People are so weary these days. Don't have much time to go beyond what their eyes can see. Too many big words and very little acceptance of what life is,' he says through his dark eyes; eyes that can speak many languages and tell many stories. I will want to stay and listen to them all because they somehow remind me of *home*.

This morning we talk briefly before I head for work. As I walk away, I realise how much brighter it all feels and looks. I smile thinking of all the *brighters* in the world; those who offer their big smiles to others as if they were greeting the God within them. The genuine joy they share is the very thing we all look for as we reach out for the divine, hoping to feel accepted and loved through our light and shadows.

Do I have what it takes to be a *brighter* myself? Do I truly see their divine self whenever I look another in the eyes? The stranger same as a loved one? Do I always remember I am standing in front of another God even when they challenge me? Even when I don't understand their choices, or I am not particularly fond of them?

As I stand on a busy train, hoping I'll get to work on time, I realise I don't always have answers to my questions because my inner wounding often gets in the way. Why would I want to brighten anyone's day if my heart aches? Why should I accept another when I don't always accept myself?

Squashed between two fellow passengers, I suddenly think that we all just want to be happy. And in that wish, we all have the same fears; fear that there won't be enough life for us to live, enough joy to feel, enough love to keep us safe.

It is our weariness that makes everybody on this carriage just a *stranger*. It is our ability to grow bigger than our own pain that enables us to offer our smiles even to those we don't know. It is our smiling eyes that remind us we have known one other all along.

Hello. Come on in. Come and sit at my table. Let's feast on life and leave nothing for later.

EVOKING GRACE.com

Nothing Ever Goes Wasted

I grew up with a pressing pain in my heart, and the worry I would always be too small in a world that often felt way too big.

I'd wake up in the middle of the night, fearing death would come and meet me before I'd had any chance to actually live. Day after day, the pain grew a bit deeper, until I buried it behind a big smile and many, many words.

To the world, I was this tiny girl with a big personality, who could talk to just anyone and was perhaps a tad *weird*. After all, a kid who goes around saying that she sees and feels *Spirit*, is meant to raise a few eyebrows.

In my heart, there was a crater the size of a field, which I could never quite fill nor I could ever walk the whole way. It felt so vast. I often wondered if anyone else had the same void inside themselves.

It was only recently that I came to accept how I had spent most of my life with what the French call *le mal de vivre*. (The literal translation is 'the pain of living.')

It sounds beautiful, doesn't it?
Le – mal – de – vivre.

Just like the title of one of those black-and-white movies, where the heroine, in the very last scene, stands on a cliff by the ocean. *Will she jump in or live on?* But life is no romance and often feels unbearable to those who are afraid to live.

And afraid I have certainly been.

When the pain became too oppressive, I slowly gave up on the façade I had been showing the world. In my *you-keep-yourself-together* personal world, that was not supposed to happen. Ever. At my end, I was meant to keep it together no matter what. There is me and me alone, while everybody else stands around, unaware of what my smile hides.

I had lived with the *malaise* long enough to know I had come to that place where the suffering heart must choose. It is the place where one gets to decide whether this life is worth their time, tears, and hope. There is no *'I'm just going to hang around and see what happens'* here anymore. You either fully give yourself to life as she is, or you simply let that void swallow you in.

'You look tired, girl! Are you sleeping OK?' My friend asks while I stand outside her front door, lost in a sea of thoughts.

I have agreed to come and spend the afternoon

with her, on the condition she does not try and offer soothing words. She has always known of my inner discomfort, and yet I sense this time she is slightly worried.

'I am fine,' I am quick to answer, hoping we will just spend our time in silence, watching life go by through the windows of her pretty house.

It is cold and grey outside, and a cup of fragrant English breakfast tea is both needed and welcomed. I take mine with no sugar and a dash of milk, and, for a moment, life feels simple and uncomplicated.

'I am happy you have come at last; look what I have just taken out of the oven.'

It's a tray full of mini scones. The heavenly smell lingers in the room, and I am ready to lose myself in a mountain of clotted cream.

I hope my friend will quickly desist from turning our encounter into some sort of I-will-save-you-from-yourself mission, while she tempts me with her gourmet skills. Thankfully, she starts talking about the importance of indulging ourselves, not just when life gets us down but especially when *she* seems to be on our side.

'You know, have a little something from time to time. A little treat. Anything that reminds us, it is not so bad after all,' she says while she pours herself some tea. 'Jam or cream first, dear?' she asks while she graciously hands me the first scone.

I look around her lovely lounge, and I suddenly remember how I have always felt at home here; safe and held in a warm embrace. Looking at the pictures of my friend with her family everywhere, I smile, knowing that there has always been much joy in this house.

'Aren't you scared you'll lose them all one day?' I ask while I reach for one of the frames.

'I will – lose – them – all – one day!' She slowly articulates every word while looking right at me. 'It does not matter whether I am scared or not. One day, all these pictures will just be a memory of a life that never stops. For anyone.'

She slowly pours herself some more tea and smiles.

'But how can you do it?' I find myself irritated by my friend's poised manners.

'Do what?'

'How can you sit here, bake your cakes, talk about your little treats, when you know that one day all this will no longer matter?'

'Will it not matter? How so?' she asks, maybe intrigued by my sudden naivety.

'Because you will have known love and then lost it all. And you will be left alone in this world. Alone. No more laughter, no more food to share, and no more hands to hold. How can you sit here pretending that your pictures make up for a life that, in the end, is just a big *fucking joke*?'

Tears are running down my cheeks now and onto my scones, while I keep on staring outside the window. Birds in the distance and trees moving in the wind; it looks like the sun may be coming out soon.

My friend keeps on biting into her scone while looking at me intently.

'There was a time when I would wake up every single morning with my heart strangled in a tight squeeze. It was hard to breathe. I thought it was ridiculous how we come so close to happiness only to have it all gone in an instant,' my friend said, not looking so cheerful now. 'Then, suddenly, one day I realised that whoever stays behind is the one who will carry the baton and then pass it on. That is all life is. Whatever love we are given, we do not hold it. We pass it on instead. To have known such great joy, no matter the inevitable ups and downs, meant that I was the recipient of something special. Truly special. How could I hold it? I had it so I could share it with others one day, for we can only share what we really made our own.

Nothing ever goes wasted, dear. We are here to pass on to others the gifts we receive along the way so this life can continue. In the end, we shall find those who left us over and over again in the eyes of the world.'

We spend the rest of the afternoon looking outside the window. With the sun no longer hidden behind the clouds, the sky is finally clear. And I, clearly, don't know life at all.

*I have been to hell and back.
And along the way I have met you.*

EVOKING GRACE.com

Strong Hands

'Come on in. Please, sit down, Antonia. How are you today?'

The woman in front of me is quite large and has a no-nonsense attitude. But there is a gentleness in her ways, which feels both reassuring and welcoming.

'My name is Anne and this lovely lady is my partner in crime, Mary.' The nurse smiles at me and I just want to cry instead.

'So Antonia, we had to bring you in because we have found quite an unusual number of suspicious cells in your cervix. At this stage, we do not want to alarm you, of course, but...' The doctor's words start to sound like an echo in the background, and this room suddenly feels very small.

I am not supposed to be here. I am not supposed to be ill because in my world that is for other people to be.

Not me.

The doctor asks me to take my underwear off and go and lie down on the bed so she can examine me and assess whether she can operate today. 'Mary will make sure you are comfortable, so this won't be too distressing for you.'

I am confused and still unsure as to why I am here. I think about the year that has gone by; about all the years spent looking for the one thing that would help me handle the insanity of this life. No matter how far I went and how hard I prayed, I never felt like I could pervert the course of life and lead her to where I thought she should go; making her turn this way and then this other way, so as to dodge the constant heartaches and uncertainties. It feels like this bed is slowly swallowing me up, and, for a moment, I would not mind disappearing. Just for one moment, I could make my excuses from this life and then come back when I can defiantly look her in the eye and say, '*Go on. Do your thing, Lady, 'cause I am not frightened of you.*'

While the doctor carefully prepares her tools and puts her gloves on, Mary, the nurse, is standing by the bed and gently puts my hand in hers. I can feel the coolness of her skin, the reassuring grasp of her fingers, and I would like her to let go of me.

'Please let me go, woman, you know nothing. If you did, you would not be so nice to me,' I think sorely to myself. But Mary, the nurse, smiles at me and now the doctor has started the small procedures that will show if I have cervical cancer. They both start talking to me to divert my attention from the pain I may soon start to feel. They make small jokes and laugh heartily, and all I can think is, why they are so caring? And why is Mary still holding my hand?

Why are these two perfect strangers being so nice to me? Surely, they must have seen thousands of women before like me. Surely a lot of them would have been in very bad shape. So why are they giving *me* so much attention? If only they knew of how I have lately been hoping for an illness that could get me out of the numbness governing my days...

'Do they die? Do many women die of this thing?' I suddenly ask, interrupting their attempt to keep me comfortable. I can feel the cold and thick tool inside of me now, and I do not like this.

'Some, but it is very rare and, at this stage, we really should not even think about this.' The nurse squeezes my hand hard while gently caressing my face.

When was the last time I held someone's hand? When did I hold another up after the inevitable falls, we all take? I do not remember; maybe never. Too busy trying to stay alive, I have made my pain bigger than the stranger's whose eyes I meet on the street. There is no time to hold others when you are wobbling around yourself.

I close my eyes while I hear these two women softly speaking to each other and tears start running down my face. I cry for all the times I hoped God would speak to me through the flames of the candle I lit, the solitude of the temples I have visited, and the mantras I have chanted.

He never did and, in the end, I remained alone

with the painful weariness of a life I seldom understood.

How do other people do it? How do they hold one another strong? How do they trust – themselves and others?

I leave the hospital that day still thinking of Mary, the nurse, and the doctor. Their strong yet gentle presence filled the room and my heart, and held me like the warmest hug.

The mothers of the world, I like calling those like them, regardless of their gender. Nurturing souls, who make us feel safe and wanted, even when we do not want ourselves. Just like a devoted mother. These are the people we all meet, along the way, when we get lost in the world; who call us *home* when it is dark outside, and we need to rest.

'Come, come and be. Come, come and rest with me,' they whisper time and time again as they hold us in their loving arms. Might it be someone close or the stranger we occasionally meet, these gracious fellow humans remind us that we are never too far from heaven? And the hell we get to live is when we forget to look into another's eyes.

A couple of months later, Anne, the doctor, calls me to announce that my biopsy has come back negative. She personally wanted to give me the good news and save me a trip to her very busy practice.

'Antonia, I want you to hear my words. Sometimes we wobble and it is OK to be scared. I felt you were trying to hold yourself together when you simply needed to rest. You do not need to prove to

anyone you have figured life out, because you have not. And you never will. So, give yourself a break and I will see you in a year's time for a checkup. I do not expect to see you any sooner for I trust you have heard my words.'

The mothers of the world, whose hands are always ready to catch us when we fall back. We heavily lean into them, trusting that soon we shall, too, hold someone else strong.

A toast to life. The mystery we are not to solve.
A toast to us. The Gods once lost, who are now reminding one another the way back home.

EVOKING GRACE.com

Miracles of Life

'I'll have a pint, please, love!'

The man standing next to me at the bar looks unsure as if he has never been in a pub in his life.

He takes the drink from the barkeeper with a grateful and timid nod.

'Oh, bugger. I am sorry. I am so sorry, love!' the man has just dropped his drink on the floor.

His first drink in a public house since the lockdown. Straight on the floor.

'Bloody lockdowns. I forgot how to be sociable,' he shyly mutters while smiling at me.

I smile back although I simply want to say, 'Me too, mate. Me too!'

The old city inn is quickly filling up, and tonight Covid-19 looks like a distant memory. Voices and laughter echo all around; the sound of glasses clinking across the room; people excitedly coming through the doors.

I have missed all this.

While the pandemic surely reinforced my appreciation for solitude, it also surprisingly rekindled my passion for life. This life; unexplainable and mysterious. Made only of a couple of certainties, and much hope and tweaking as we go along.

'What can I get you, babes?' the friendly barmaid asks while I wait for my husband and our dog to arrive.

Sitting at the bar is a good way to people-watch while contemplating life.

'I'll have a bottle of house red and a couple of glasses, please. Oh, and some crips too!' I quickly say, remembering how wine and crisps are the perfect combo for a lazy Saturday afternoon.

'Is that an amethyst you've got there, babes?' the girl asks, pointing at my necklace.

'Oh yes, it's an old favourite of mine.'

'It suits ya. You look very spiritual, love!'

'Why is that?' I ask teasingly, half expecting a tentative description of what spiritual folks look like.

'You know, the whole look. The accessories, the clothes, the whole thing. You look *zen!*' the chatty barmaid assuredly explains.

I smile and thank her while I feel a hand gently resting on my shoulder. I always love it when my husband does that.

'Do I look zen?'

'What do you mean?'

'Do I look zen to you? The girl behind the bar said that I do!'

'What does that even mean?' Warren asks,

looking confused and not sure what I'm really asking.

'Dunno...enlightened, perhaps?' I jokingly say, trying to get more out of him.

Instead, he laughs and suggests we crack open the wine and enjoy the crisps. 'Uh, I love salt and vinegar! Thank you, baby,' he says while wrapping his arm around me.

Our dog is now licking my ankle, so I pick her up onto my lap while my husband pours the wine.

From our corner at the bar, the rest of the pub looks busy and, for once, I welcome being among company. While we normally enjoy the quieter and more hidden venues, tonight the lively crowd is a reminder of what we all have in common: *life.*

Regardless of the choices we make during our time in this world, we are the *carriers of life.* We simply do not remember that. *Miracles of life* in constant creation, we drift away from what we really are. As we enter this world, we fall under an ancient spell that causes us to forget what pulsates in our veins.

'Where do I come from? Who am I? Where will I be going next?' are questions we will all be asking ourselves, at some point or another.

Some of us go and look for the answers in the far-reaching corners of the world. They retreat in deep solitude, away from our mundane comforts, making themselves available for something bigger to speak and reveal the truths of life. Others build communities and bring together many people, trying to offer meaning and purpose to what often leaves us baffled and unsure.

While our search always takes us away from ourselves, we seem reluctant to stay close instead; within our hearts; as if life could only happen far in the distance. Maybe if our search ended, we would no longer need to ask questions for we never really needed answers. Perhaps we are simply afraid to remember, and our quest is a mere distraction from what we have known and learnt to forget; *that we are the very thing we hope will answer our prayers.*

In this busy pub, in a frantic and loud metropolis, God is as present as It is in the solitude of a sacred site. It is in the laughter and loud voices of the people standing all around us; same as in the invocations echoing within quiet chapels. A God that we often do not understand, become suspicious of, and are not always fond of.

With our answers hidden in the struggle to accept our divinity, we look up at the sky in the hope of making sense of what is down here. We remember that we are God only when we learn to live in the unknown unfolding of our existence, seeing our reflections all around; especially in what feels unacceptable and alien.

'What are you thinking of, my love?' My husband asks while our dog now licks my hand. Her tiny tongue on my skin is one of the joys that never fails to make me smile.

'Nothing much. I'm just enjoying the wine and the lovely company. Fancy more crisps?'

'You are here, at last. What took you so long? I have been looking for you all over!' God looks up at me surprised... 'I was close. Very close. Just out of sight. So you could find yourself first.'

EVOKING GRACE.com

Afterword

This book has been in the making for a long time. A lifetime perhaps.

It was never meant to be a book about religion and faith but instead about people – the ones we love and lose; the ones we cross paths with for five seconds or who remain in our lives for eternity; and the people whose choices we often do not understand, but who are closer to us than we would like to admit. *For, in the end, we are all gods playing humans*. It's a game not always fair and certainly not for the faint-hearted soul. In this life, we take on different roles, always aiming in the same direction. And, as we approach the finish line, we remember that we saw God in one another's eyes all along.

Reflecting on what the three Covid years have meant to all of us, one would wonder what keeps us going at times of upheaval. How can we really look forward to a new dawn when the night never seems to end? These are times when both spiritual and mundane feel like a palliative distraction from the simple truth we find hard to accept.

Why do we keep going? We fall, we stop and then fall again. Nevertheless, we get going.

Why?

Because we are here to live.

Life does not stop. It simply transforms, as we get to die a zillion times, and a zillion times we are reborn. What we were yesterday is not what we are in this moment, and, unbeknownst to us, we always anticipate that new dawn. Even when it appears otherwise, we are in fact choosing life. Even the most unlikely choice, is an attempt to remain here, fully immersed in what often feels like an impenetrable mystery.

To truly accept our divine origins, is to let the mystery be unsolved. As we feel its sacredness, we no longer desperately try to crack the code. Instead, we become it. We become the very thing we have tried so hard to grasp, and yet we never could.

Dear Reader, I hope my stories have left you smiling and warmed your heart. And, if you are ever in a pub, I hope you'll want to pass this little book on to other people too. It is my sincere wish that you start to see how precious your own stories are as well. Share them with others with an open heart, knowing that this way you grow bigger than your own wounds. As you grow, the whole world grows with you.

May you dwell in the sacredness of your days. May you feel your vastness in the solitude of your heart and when standing next to another, may you remember that they are God, also.

Afterword

With much love and grace from my heart to yours,

Antonia Lyons

About the Author

I was born in 1974, in a small Italian town on the Jonico Sea, which had once been a jewel of the Greek empire.

I have always been a sensitive and intuitive, and since a very young age called to open to the soulful realms.

It was after having a prophetic dream that I knew it was time to leave the Italian sunny skies. In my dream, my late grandmother, who once had been the wise woman and healer of her village, told me that there was much I would find down the misty alleys of London. Whatever that might be, she urged me to share it with others and ready my-self for the man mI would continue my journey with.

I landed in the British capital with only fifty quid in my pocket, moved around a lot for a while, lost my way a couple of times, and eventually settled down in the heart of London.

Today I share my life with my husband Warren and our adorable Coton de Tulear, Zhibbi. I am an *Intuitive Storyteller* and the founder of Evoking-grace.com, an online platform designed to inspire others to reconnect to their own wisdom and tune into the creative flow moving within them. My popular 'Intuitive Storytelling,' offers healing words to those looking to find language for what wishes to emerge through their endless stories.